D0689923

MAKING MUSICAL THINGS

CHARLES SCRIBNER'S SONS
New York

MAKING MUSICAL THINGS

IMPROVISED INSTRUMENTS

Ann Wiseman

Copyright © 1979 Ann Wiseman

Library of Congress Cataloging in Publication Data
Wiseman, Ann.
Making musical things.
SUMMARY: Includes directions for constructing a
variety of musical instruments from easily obtainable
materials such as milk cartons and embroidery hoops.
1. Musical instruments—Juvenile literature.
2. Musical instruments—Construction. [1. Musical
instruments—Construction. 2. Handicraft] 1. Title.
ML3930.A2W6   781.9′6   79-4474
ISBN 0-684-16114-1

Charles Scribner's Sons
Macmillan Publishing Company
866 Third Avenue, New York, NY 10022
Collier Macmillan Canada, Inc.

Printed in the United States of America
7 9 11 13 15 17 19 MD/C 20 18 16 14 12 10 8

Ideas, credits, and thanks to: The many people who invented, explored, and created
musical instruments at The Boston Children's Museum when I was there, and the 1972-
73 staff of the Advisory for Open Education in Cambridge, Massachusetts—especially
Cornelia Voorhees. The Education Development Center, and Dan Watt and Emily
Romney of the Elementary Science Study who conceived the Musical Instruments
Recipe Book and Whistles and Strings published by McGraw-Hill. Jack Langstaff, Paul
Earls, Mariagnese Knill-Cattaneo, and Suzanne Pearce for helpful suggestions. Carl von
Mertens for instrument building help. Bonney Laurie Rega, Vanessa Kirsch, and Sarah
Bartholomew for posing with instruments so I could draw them. Doug Lipman for his
bibliography. Mills & Boon Ltd., for permission to reproduce the scale on page 39, from
Making Musical Instruments by Peter Williams. Albert Whitman & Company for the
random pipes made from garden hose described on page 39, adapted from Music and
Instruments for Children to Make by John Hawkinson & Martha Faulhaber, copyright
© 1969 by Albert Whitman & Company.

CONTENTS

Things to make
Sounds to hear
Swell the heart
Excite the ear
Clap the hands
Tap the feet
Swing the hips
Catch the beat
Gather the children
In the street
Soothe the shepherd
Calm the sheep
Put the babies
Fast to sleep

Create your song
Follow your dream
Use your mood
Sing your name
Rhyme your age
Tap your street
Give the rhythm
to your feet
Fill the air
Bow the string
Every person
has a theme
Where ever you are
We're listening
love Ann.

FEELINGS...MINE...YOURS...

EMOTION. EXPRESSION. RHYTH

TRANSPORTATION. INTERNATIONAL. LANGUA

READING AND WRITING --oo

MOTION ...oo... STRUCTURE ...

MUSIC

LOVE

EXPERIMENTATION

HARMONICS

SOUND.... SONG

REVERBERATION

SYNCOPATION

COUNTER . POINT

MEASURE AND MATH

PROGRESSION

BEAT

HAND SKILLS AND DEXTERITY

PASSION

NON-SCALE

FREEDOM

SCALE &

CREATION

COMPOSITION

COMMUNICATION

JOY

UNITY

TTENTION

OURS

KITCHEN THINGS THAT RING

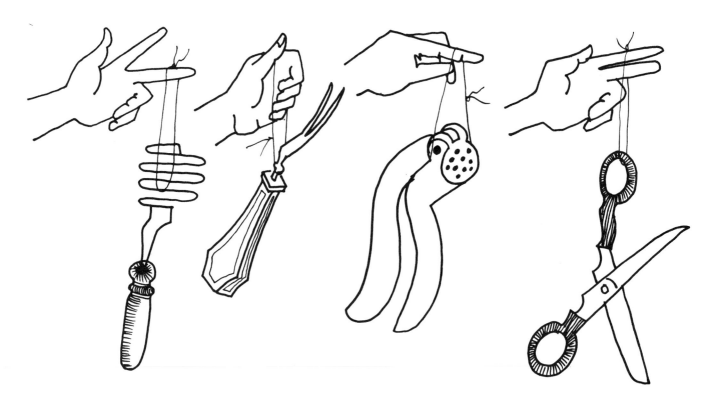

look around the kitchen,
hang utensils from a string,
tap them with a pencil
to see if they ring.

& PING

rest a fork on the plastic lid
of an empty coffee can—
ping the prongs with your fingernails
to hear the fork sing.

BELLS · CHIMES · TRIANGLE

stemmed wine glasses
rubbed with a wet finger
around the lip edge sing.

water glasses filled
to diminishing levels
tapped with a spoon

clay flower pots hung from a rod
(try different sizes)
strike gently with a stick —
(a cracked pot won't ring.)

bells sewn on a ribbon or elastic
to be worn on legs and arms

unpainted metal coat hangers
hanging from a stick
when struck with a nail sing.

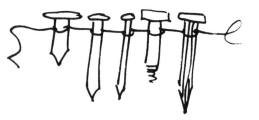

house nails chime
when tied together.
strike with a nail.

the sound of a triangle
can be had from a fork
or from a nail or bent steel.

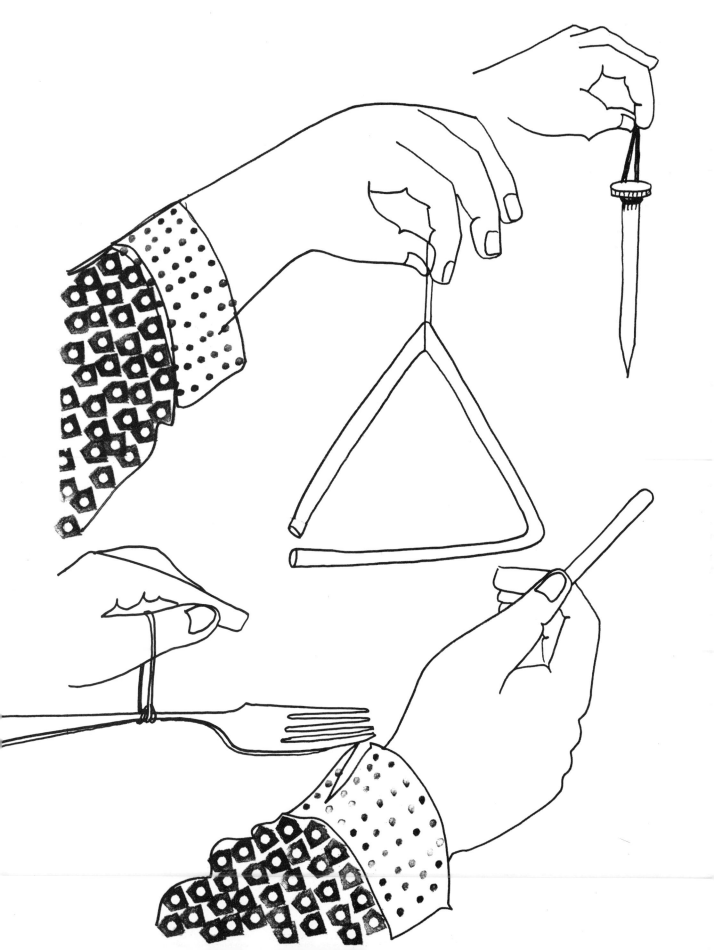

SCRAPERS & RASPS

LOOK AROUND THE KITCHEN

strum a pancake flipper.

scrape a cheese grater
with a stick or a pencil.

GUIRO

FROM LATIN AMERICA

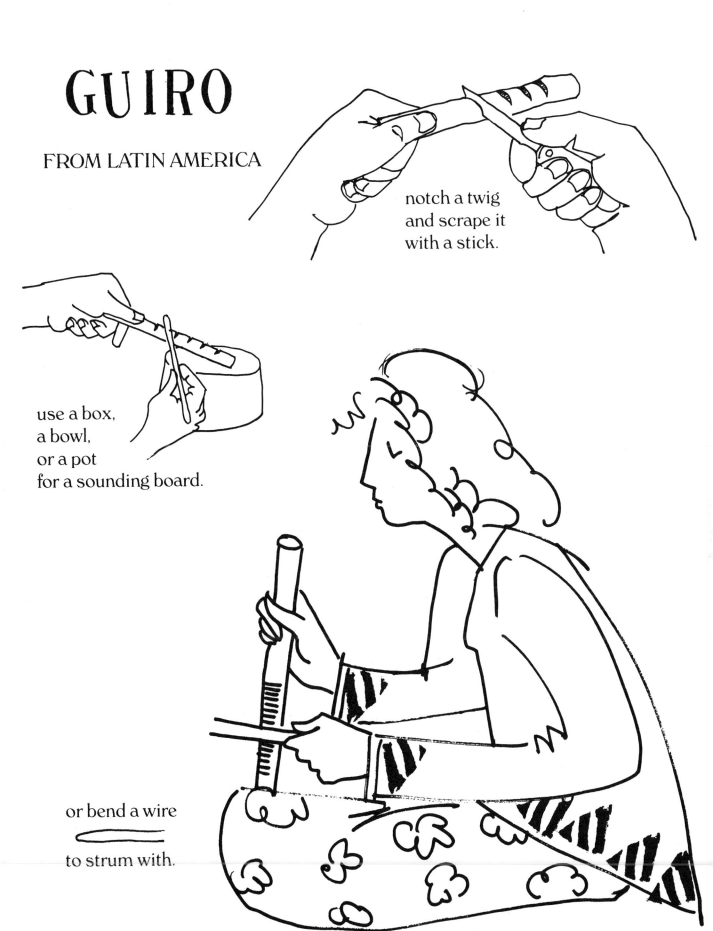

notch a twig
and scrape it
with a stick.

use a box,
a bowl,
or a pot
for a sounding board.

or bend a wire

to strum with.

TAMBOURINE

aluminum pie pan

2 paper soup bowls glued together
like a rattle with pebbles inside
or clappers sewn on the edges

hoops made of cardboard,
heavy belt leather,
flexible plastic

try wooden or plastic hoops.
drill or poke holes with a hot nail.
thread clappers or tie them on.

stretch thin hide, rubber inner tubing,
canvas, or fabric over hoops to make a head.
(after fabric is stretched over hoop
saturate with diluted Elmer's glue to give
head a better tone and tightness.)

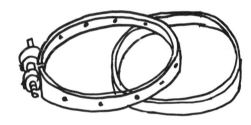

try embroidery hoops.
(stretch hide or chamois skin
over the smaller hoop and
secure with the larger hoop)

clappers can be made out of sea shells,
screw eyes, buttons, washers, coins with
holes, or bottle caps flattened with a hammer.

CLAPPERS

REMOVE INNER CORK

tap a big loose
hole in each of the caps
and thread
them on a wire
or a paper clip.

DRUM IMPROVISATIONS

fabric sized with glue makes a good drum head—
so do rubber bed sheets or inner tubing.

 * head

coffee can
with plastic lid
on one end or both

canvas or plastic
stretched over tin
or wooden bowl
taped tight or tied
with elastic or string

coconut or gourd
with plastic, cloth,
or hide
stretched over
tightly and tied

cut a section of
paper core tubing.
make a cardboard
or wooden top,
or use an ice cream barrel.

2-HEADED DRUM
remove top and bottom
from large vegetable cans
found at schools.
stretch cloth,
rubber, or hide
over openings.
stitch round each head.
lash the stitches top to bottom.

waste basket
or garbage pail
with stretched canvas

steel oil drum
top section, into
which sound pockets
can be hammered

empty gallon plastic milk jugs
turned upside down

DRUM STICKS

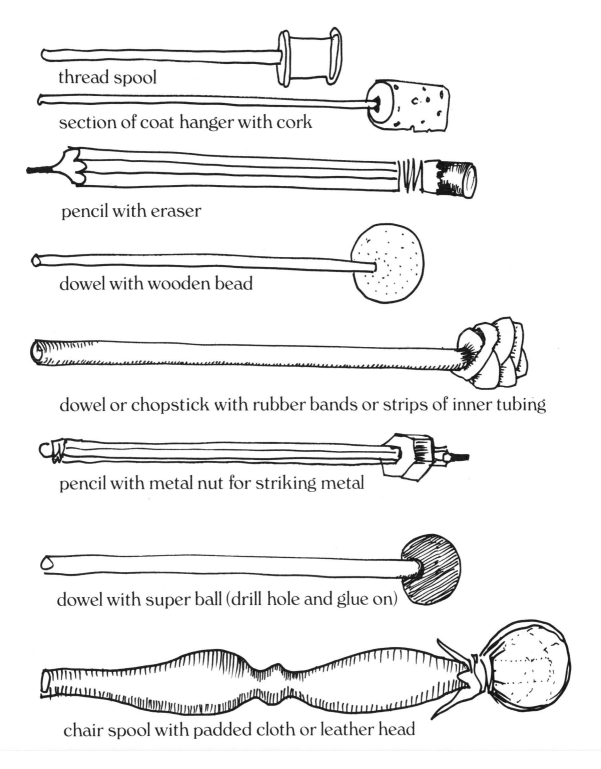

thread spool

section of coat hanger with cork

pencil with eraser

dowel with wooden bead

dowel or chopstick with rubber bands or strips of inner tubing

pencil with metal nut for striking metal

dowel with super ball (drill hole and glue on)

chair spool with padded cloth or leather head

BRAZING RODS

you need about 25 low fuming
bronze brazing rods 1/16″ diameter.
available at welding suppliers

1. cut 8″, 9″,10″, 11″, 12″, 13″, 14″, 15″ lengths.
   drill scant 1/16″ holes in 2″ x 4″ block of wood
   seat rods tightly 3/4″ to 1″ deep into block
   (use pliers).
   (the tighter the fit the clearer the sound)
   to hear richer tones, set block on sound box.
   tap rod close to the footing with pencil.

2. cut a "forest" of rods uniform lengths.
   (try 14″ lengths)
   seat them in a wood block
   to hear them ring.
   strum, tap, or brush them.

drill
hole
and
solder

p.s. tuning rods to scale is
difficult but possible.
richer, deeper notes can be made
by soldering 3/16″ rod sections onto 1/16″ legs.
guidance is needed for use of drill press,
propane torch, and solder.

these ideas were inspired by Harry Bertoia's sound sculptures

POT COVERS

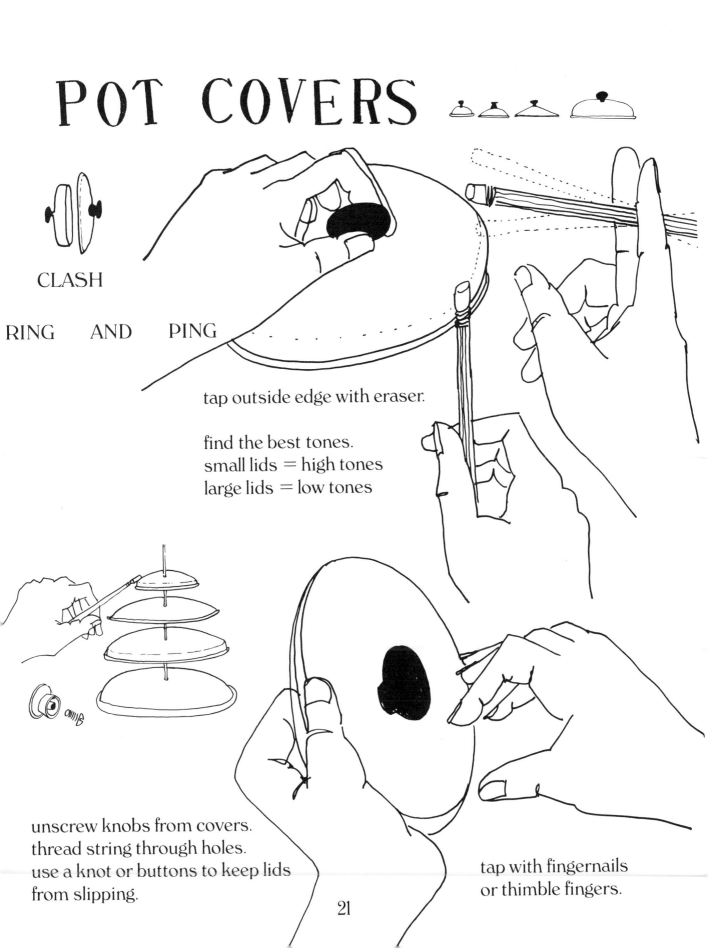

CLASH

RING   AND   PING

tap outside edge with eraser.

find the best tones.
small lids = high tones
large lids = low tones

unscrew knobs from covers.
thread string through holes.
use a knot or buttons to keep lids
from slipping.

tap with fingernails
or thimble fingers.

CRYING WATER BOWLS & COOKING POTS

stainless steel bowls with 1/2 cup of water swirling around when struck on the bottom make strange sounds.

tin pans and rice pots ring and sing when struck.
swirling water distorts the note and carries the sound.

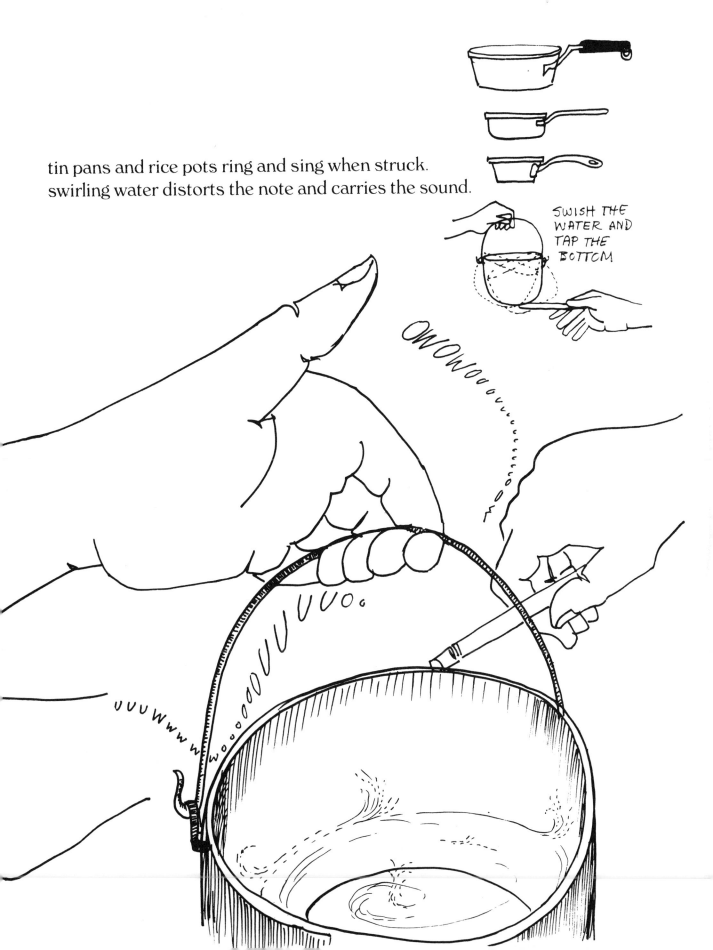

SWISH THE
WATER AND
TAP THE
BOTTOM

RATTLE & CLATTER

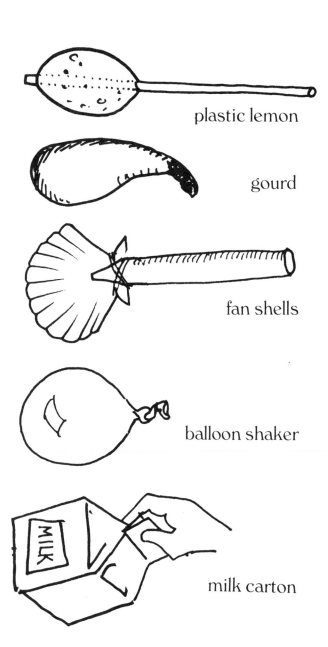

plastic lemon

gourd

fan shells

balloon shaker

milk carton

rattle bones
(short or spare ribs)

any empty container:
plastic, wood, paper,
glass, cardboard or gourd
filled with stones,
rice, beans, peas, sand, etc.

split dowel tip to hold
the shells together.

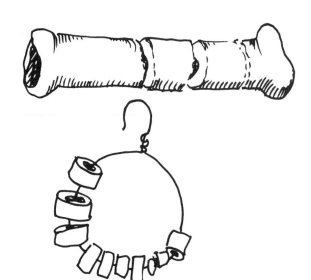

bones threaded on a
rounded coat hanger clatter!

sew wire through
a plastic mailing tube,
making a maze
for rice or dried peas
or sand to run through.
(instead of wire,
 poke pins or nails in tube.)

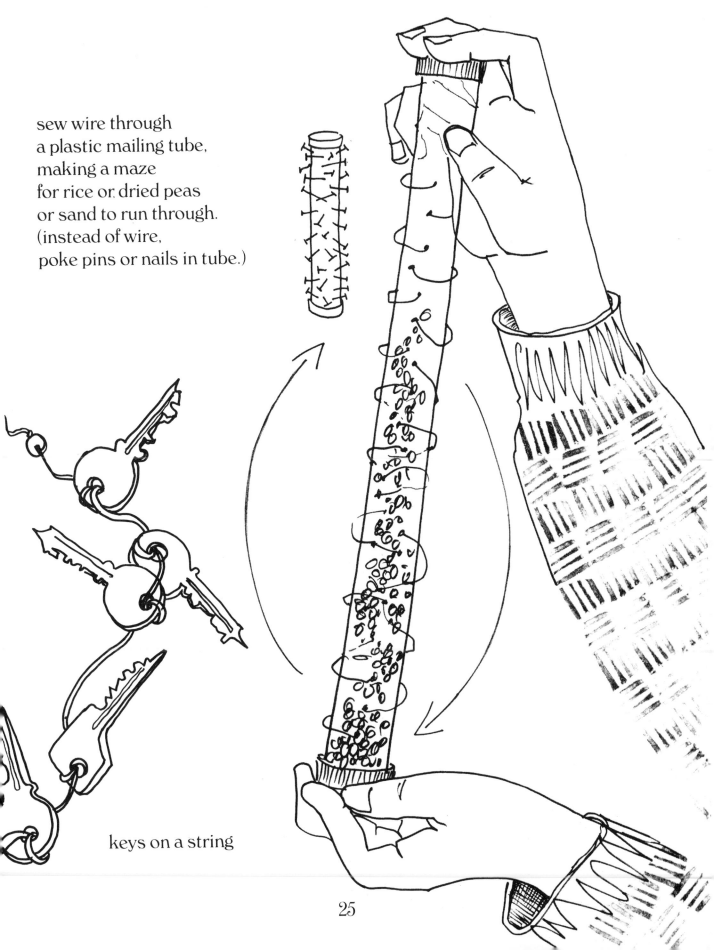

keys on a string

THIMBLE FINGERS
& TAPPING GLOVES

buy 10 thimbles that fit tight.
metal or plastic is all right.
tap on wood, tap on stone
tap on metal, tap on bone.
every surface has a sound.

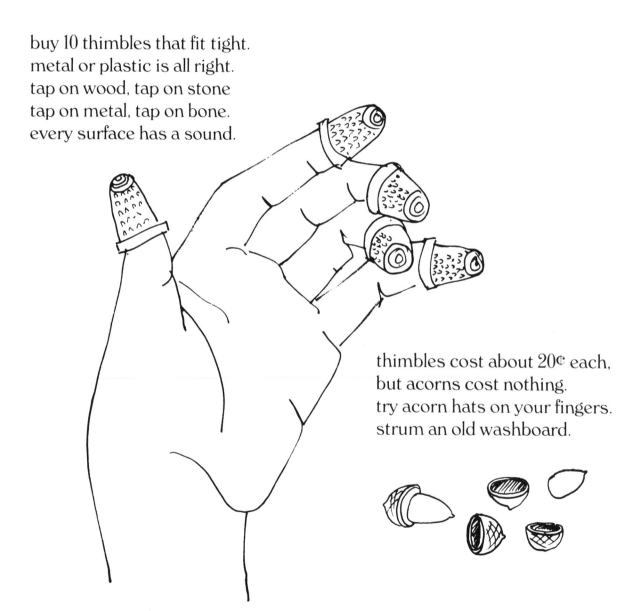

thimbles cost about 20¢ each,
but acorns cost nothing.
try acorn hats on your fingers.
strum an old washboard.

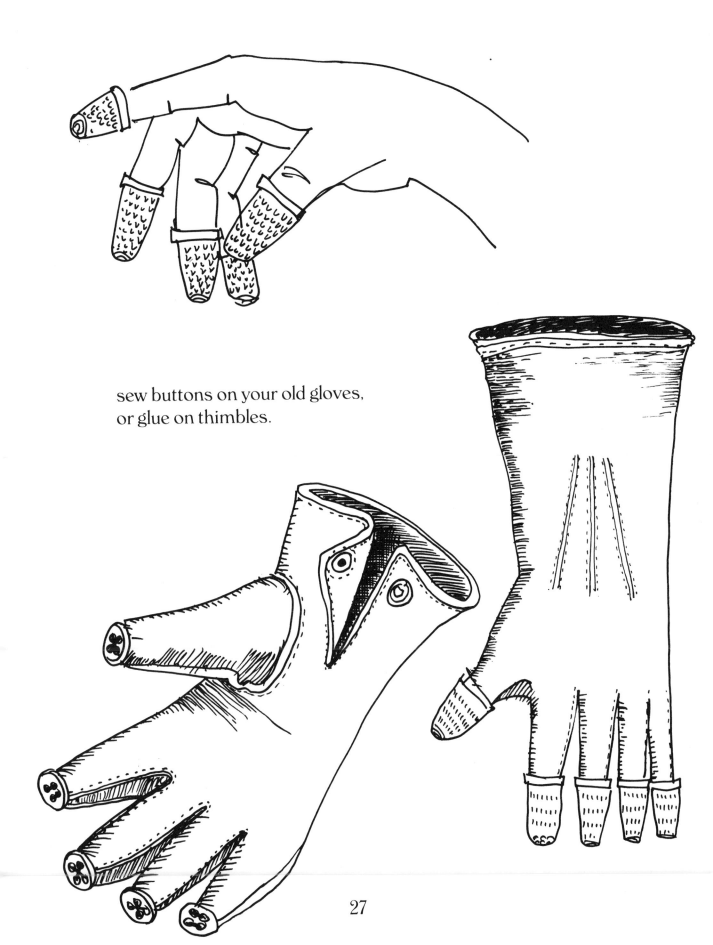

sew buttons on your old gloves,
or glue on thimbles.

CLAVE & RHYTHM STICKS

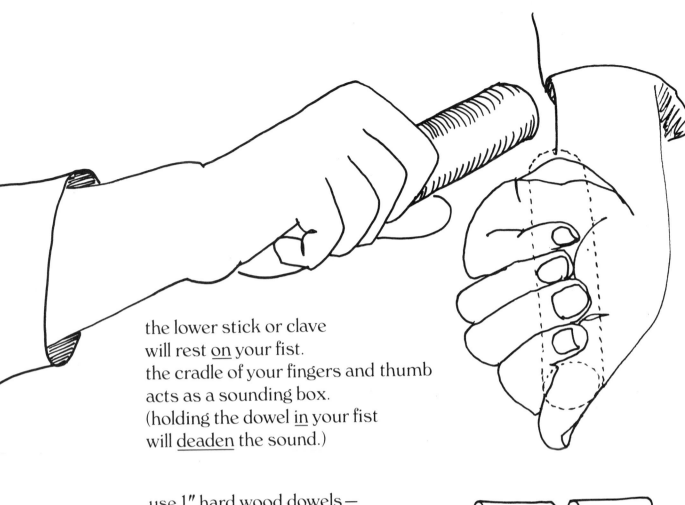

the lower stick or clave
will rest _on_ your fist.
the cradle of your fingers and thumb
acts as a sounding box.
(holding the dowel _in_ your fist
will _deaden_ the sound.)

use 1" hard wood dowels —
any length easy to hold (4" or 5" long).

SAND BLOCKS

tack sandpaper on wooden blocks.
tack on tape or ribbon as hand holders.

LAGERPHON

shake
your
stick
or tap
it
on
the
ground.

JINGLING
JOHNNY

use a thick broomstick and some thin nails with heads.
flatten bottle caps with hammer.
make big nail holes in bottle caps
so caps will clap and slide on nail easily.

HAND
HOLD

slip 2 or more caps
on each nail
then hammer into
broom stick.
leave a section
free of nails
for the hand hold.
put a rubber
chair coaster
or crutch cap
on one end
so you can
tap stick
on the ground.

CONDUIT PIPE XYLOPHONE

conduit pipe usually comes in 10′ lengths.
it costs about $2.00 per length.
you will also need about 3′ of felt weather stripping.

small set — use 10′ of 1/2″ electrical conduit pipe
large set — use 20′ of 1/2″ electrical conduit pipe

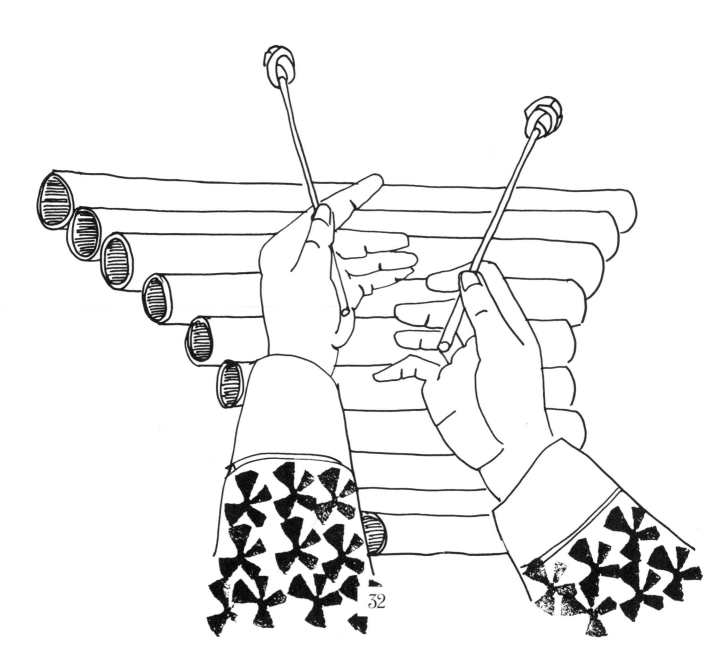

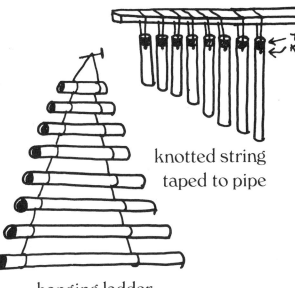

knotted string
taped to pipe

hanging ladder

make rack of wood,
styrofoam, rubber,
or felt strips.

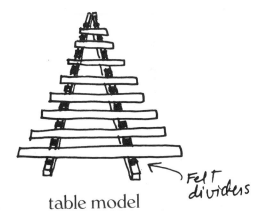

table model

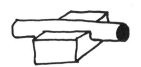

styrofoam cradle

individual styrofoam
pipe cradle

ask for EMT, found in hardware stores and lumber yards (copper pipe is more expensive but easier to cut and has a richer tone).

1. cut the longest pipe first.
   in case you lose this note
   by cutting the bar too short
   you can use the "mistake"
   for the next note and nothing is wasted.
   filing the pipe end heightens the note.
   (it helps if you have a good ear for tone.)

2. cut 2 one-foot lengths
   of felt weather stripping.
   then cut 11 one-half inch felt divider pads.
   glue pads between pipes so pipes don't roll.
   or, you can cut ditches in styrofoam blocks,
   or make each note bar an individual cradle,
   or, you can tie the pipes into a hanging ladder.

measurements*

		large	small
low	so	22 7/16″	11 7/32″
low	la	21 1/4″	10 5/8″
low	ti	20″	10″
	do	19 1/2″	9 3/4″
	re	18 1/4″	9 1/8″
	mi	17 1/8″	8 9/16″
	fa	16 5/8″	8 5/16″
	so	15 5/8″	7 13/16″
	la	14 3/4″	7 3/8″
	ti	13 3/4″	6 7/8″
high	do	13 7/16″	6 23/32″

*Reproduced from the Musical Instrument Recipe Book by permission of the Elementary Science Study of Education Development Center, Inc.

WOODEN XYLOPHONE

go to a lumberyard with a pencil.
tap different kinds of wood—
some of them really sing.
try redwood, fruitwood, mahogany, hardwoods.
to make a rack to hold note bars
use wood or styrofoam
or 2 lengths of felt weather stripping
or, tie your bars into a ladder.
hang it up or lay it down.

Tuning wooden bars can be tricky
if you get discouraged,
why not settle for a set
of random notes . . .
and invent your own new sounds.

The Moldavian monk sounds the plank

cut 8 or more tones.
tuning can be random
or scaled.
these measurements are approximate.
use 7/8″ x 7/8″ wood.
Columbian pine or hard sonorous woods
make the best tone.

do is C

low	so	14 1/4″
low	la	13 1/2″
low	ti	12 7/8″
	do	12 1/8″
	re	11 1/2″
	mi	10 3/4″
	fa	10 1/4″
	so	9 5/8″
	la	9 1/4″
	ti	8 1/2″
high	do	8 3/8″
high	re	7 3/4″
high	mi	7 3/8″
high	fa	7 1/8″
high	so	6 3/4″

rack   Felt strips

to heighten a note,
sand or saw off a sliver from the end.
to lower a note,
saw a shallow notch into the block.

The above measurements are from Ronald Roberts' book
<u>Musical Instruments Made to Be Played</u> published by
Dryad Press, Woodridge, New Jersey.

BUGLES & HORNS

I heard someone actually play a christmas song on this tube!

one or more
yards of
shower hose or
flexible tubing

shower bulb
mouthpiece
(—better yet,
find one from
an old trumpet.)

tin funnel

WIND TUBE
plastic pool tubing (1″ diameter)
when swung around and around fast
makes many notes...an amazing sound.

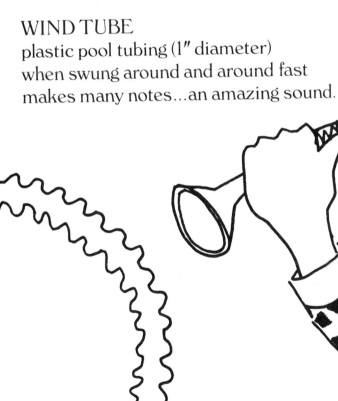

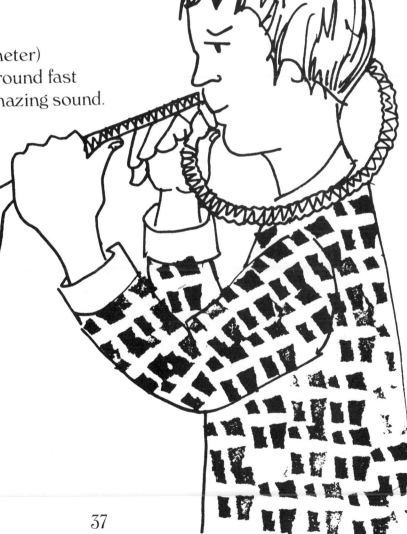

RANDOM PIPES

cut a bunch of plastic straws different lengths
or use 1/2"-3/4" plastic tubing
or, use cane cut in random lengths.
plug the bottoms of the tubes with Plasticine—
the higher you put the plug, the higher the note.
(push plug in with a pencil or nail head.)

lash pipes together as the shepherds do
with string, tape, or thong.

blow across the tops.
(it takes a little practice.)

short tubes = high notes
long tubes = low notes

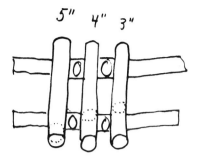

TEST-TUBE PIPES
diminish the water
vary the tones
add vegetable color
so small people can play a tune
by reading a color chart.

1. cut with scissors 3 pieces
   garden hose, each 5" long.
   plug with Plasticine.
2. plug one piece at one end.
   plug second piece at 4" length.
   plug third piece at 3" length.
   (use a pencil to push in the Plasticine.)
3. lay pipes on 2 strips of masking tape.
   put a pinch of Plasticine between
   each pipe. then wrap around.
   blow across the top.*

*from Hawkinson & Faulhaber: <u>Music and Instruments for Children to Make</u>. Albert Whitman & Co.

try diminishing sizes of plastic straws.
stick straws in a section of
corrugated box or Tri-wall.
glue straws in place.
tape bottoms shut or plug with Plasticine.

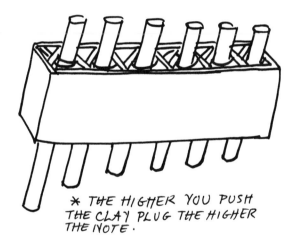

* THE HIGHER YOU PUSH THE CLAY PLUG THE HIGHER THE NOTE.

if you want to get a proper Western scale, try:

Do	(C)	= 6 3/4"
Re	(D)	= 6"
Mi	(E)	= 5 1/4"
Fa	(F)	= 4 3/4"
So	(G)	= 4 1/4"
La	(A)	= 3 3/4"
Ti	(B)	= 3 1/2"
Do	(C)	= 3 1/4"

RECORDERS & FLUTES

pipes, recorders, and flutes
can be made out of bamboo,
cane, plastic drinking straws, test-tubes,
garden hose, papier mâché,
empty ball point pen tubes.

remember,
primitive pipes
come in all sizes
with unscaled notes.
with that freedom
you can explore sound
that interests the ears.

SHEPHERDS' PIPES

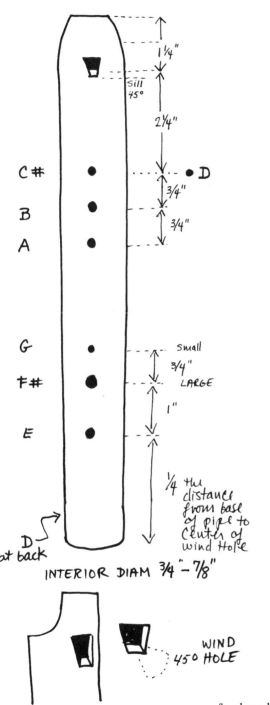

1 1/4"

Sill 45°

2 1/4"

C# • • D

3/4"

B

3/4"

A

G — Small 3/4"

F# — LARGE

1"

E

1/4 the distance from base of pipe to center of wind hole

D at back

INTERIOR DIAM 3/4" – 7/8"

WIND HOLE 45°

use a section of bamboo
about 11 1/2" long x 3/4" or 7/8" diameter
or try plastic pipe
or a papier mâché tube
formed around a broom stick.

find or shape a cork that fits the opening.
drill or burn holes.
don't forget the wind hole
and the thumb hole (D)
on the back directly behind C.

1/3"

3/4"

1/2"

←1/4→

3/16"

1 1/4"

CUT CORK

CUT THE CHANNEL INSIDE THE MOUTH PIECE

for bamboo pipes that are more precise,
see Margaret Galloway's book <u>Making</u> <u>and</u> <u>Playing</u> <u>Bamboo Pipes</u>
published by Dryad Press, Woodbridge, New Jersey.

CASTANETS & CLAPPERS

SPOONS
wood or metal, clapped together,
make a good hollow sound.

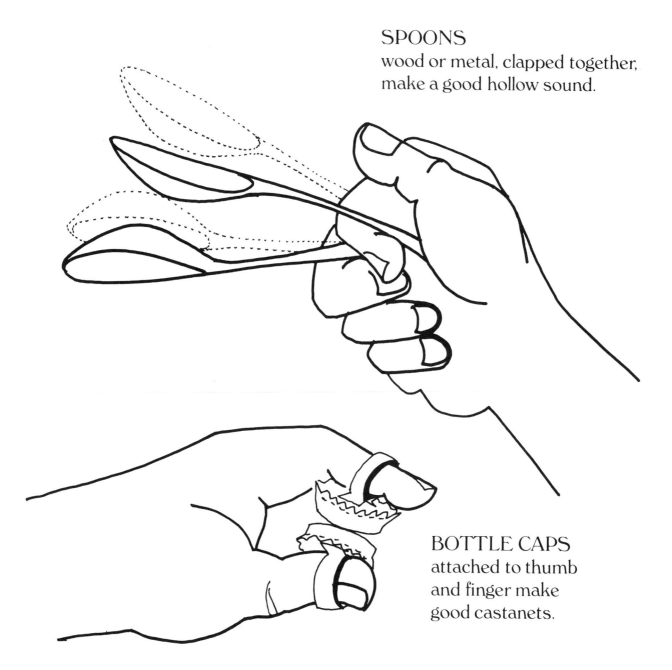

BOTTLE CAPS
attached to thumb
and finger make
good castanets.

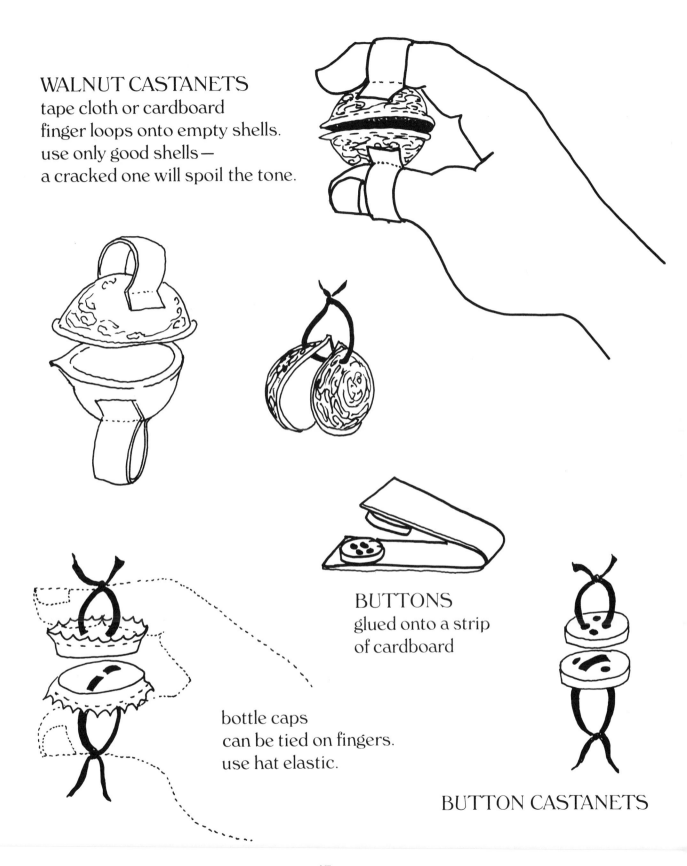

WALNUT CASTANETS
tape cloth or cardboard
finger loops onto empty shells.
use only good shells—
a cracked one will spoil the tone.

BUTTONS
glued onto a strip
of cardboard

bottle caps
can be tied on fingers.
use hat elastic.

BUTTON CASTANETS

BOARD & BOX ZITHER

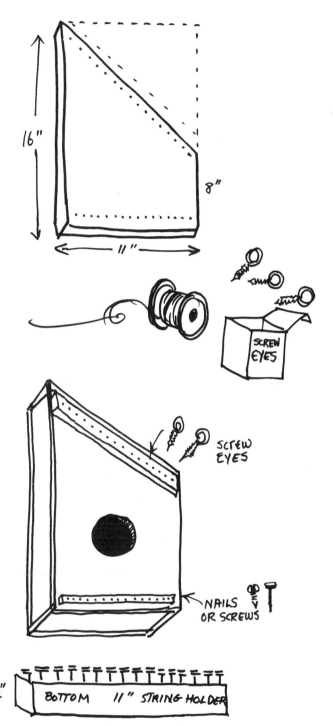

THE SIMPLE BOARD ZITHER
cut a 1" board 16" x 11" x 8",
more or less.
1" in from left side
mark dots with pencil
every 1/2" at bottom for nails.
at top along the angle
mark dots every 3/4"
for screw-eye string tighteners.

THE BOX ZITHER
make a thin wooden box 16" x 11" x 8",
using sonorous wood like cherry,
redwood, maple, cedar, or spruce.
for the sounding board top.
the rest of the box can be anything
you happen to have handy, like pine.

cut a sound hole
approximately 3" in diameter
in the lower center of the box.
cut two strips of wood—
a 13 1/2" strip for the top to hold
the screw-eye string tighteners,
and an 11" strip
for the bottom string holder.
glue strips to sounding board.
string with guitar gut,
squidding line, or nylon monofilament.
tune with the help of a piano.

P.S. you can also make
a 3-octave zither
or a 4-octave table model.

45

ONE-STRING
BOX BASS

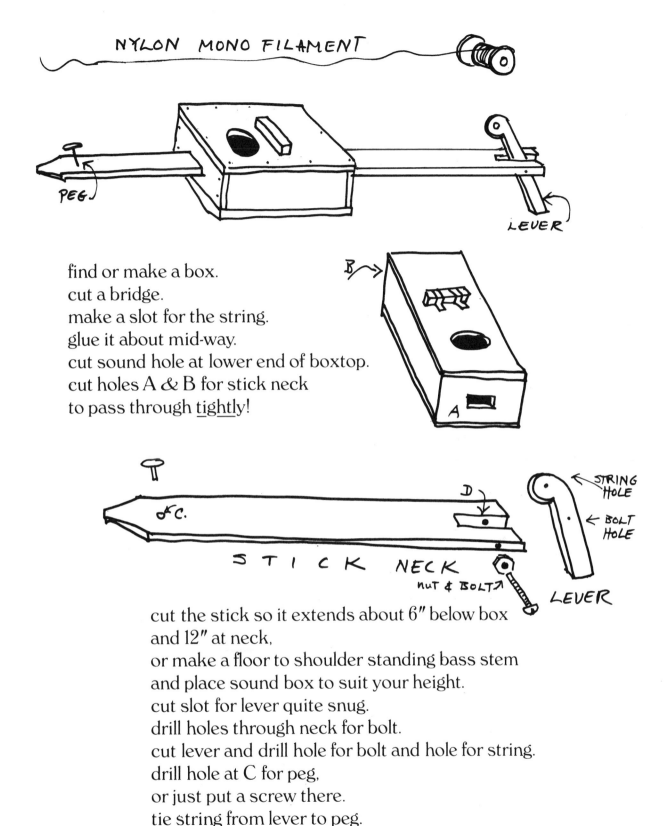

NYLON MONO FILAMENT

PEG

LEVER

find or make a box.
cut a bridge.
make a slot for the string.
glue it about mid-way.
cut sound hole at lower end of boxtop.
cut holes A & B for stick neck
to pass through <u>tightly</u>!

B

A

STRING HOLE

BOLT HOLE

ofC.

D

STICK NECK

NUT & BOLT

LEVER

cut the stick so it extends about 6″ below box
and 12″ at neck,
or make a floor to shoulder standing bass stem
and place sound box to suit your height.
cut slot for lever quite snug.
drill holes through neck for bolt.
cut lever and drill hole for bolt and hole for string.
drill hole at C for peg,
or just put a screw there.
tie string from lever to peg.
pull lever handle down to change sound.
and pluck or use bow for different sounds.

BUSHMAN'S BOW · LYRE · RUBBER BAND BOX · TIN CAN HARP

the Bushmen
of the Kalihari
make their bows sing
by tapping
the arrow shaft
against the string.

The Africans have taught us
new sounds - . . . . just listen!

rubber bands sing
across a firm box.
raise bands up on pencils.
wrap rubber bands or straps
around the back or legs of a chair
and strum.

the Nuba of Africa
play a variety of 5-string lyre
and an arc bow — strung across the top
and down to the arc — giving 2 tones.

invent your own lyre.
try a Y branch
or a can with bent wires
for plucking,
bowing, or tapping.
for string
try strips of
stretch rubber bands,
gut, fishing line,
or nylon monofilament.

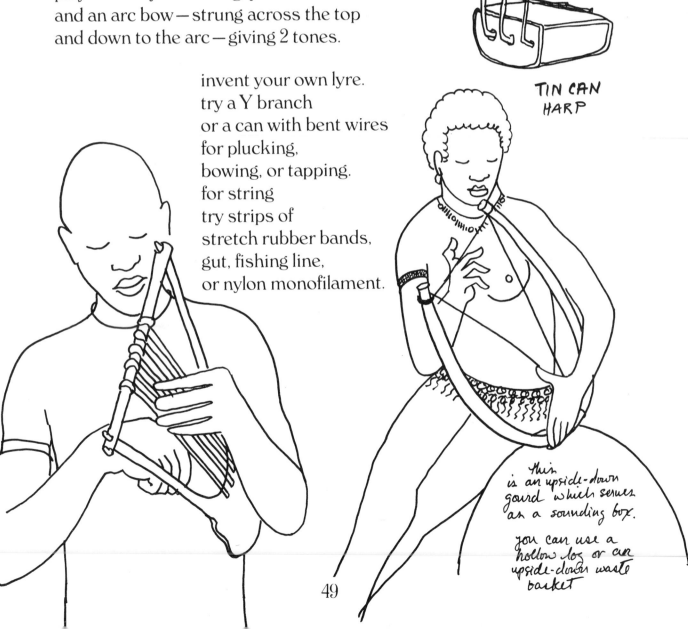

KLEENEX

TIN CAN
HARP

this
is an upside-down
gourd which serves
as a sounding box.

you can use a
hollow log or an
upside-down waste
basket

49

THUMB PIANOS
KALIMBA · IMBIRA · KAFFIR

cut a coconut in half.
drink the milk.
eat the meat without breaking the shell.
cut a wooden disk a little larger
than the shell opening and taper the
edges so it fits tightly into the coconut.

wire tongues can be made out of hammered
umbrella stays, or try flattened coat
hanger wire of different lengths,
or "cut-nails" flattened.

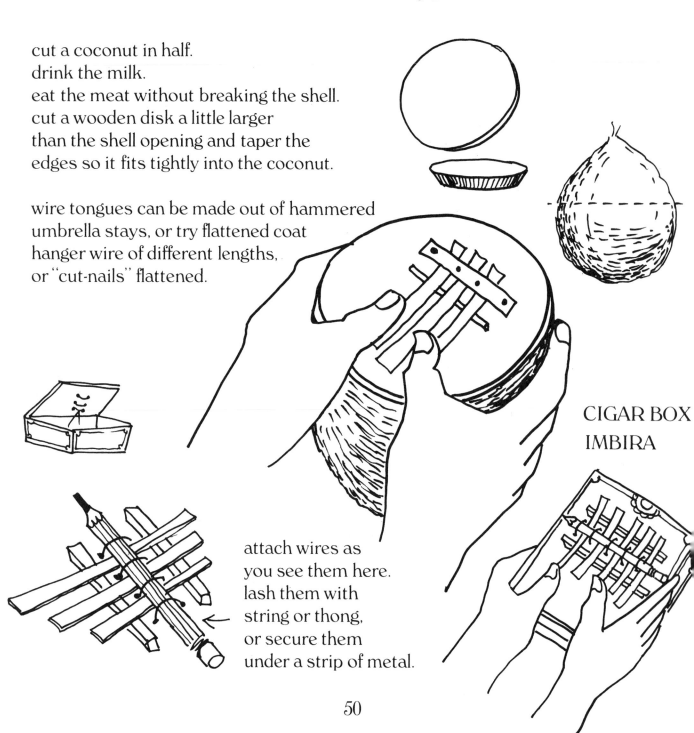

CIGAR BOX
IMBIRA

attach wires as
you see them here.
lash them with
string or thong,
or secure them
under a strip of metal.

SHINGLE PLUNKER

sand a shingle smooth.
(cedar is best.)
cut it in half.
place thin end on top
and thick end on bottom.
cut teeth in diminishing lengths.

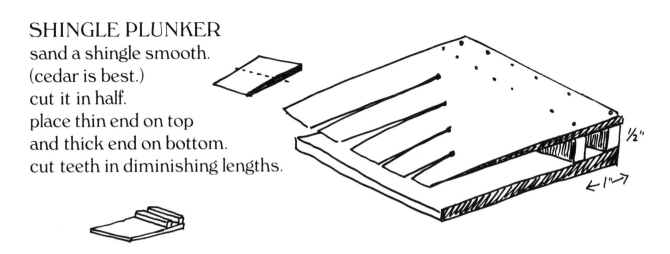

nail two thin strips
at thick end of bottom piece.
attach top to strips.

SARDINE CAN KALIMBA

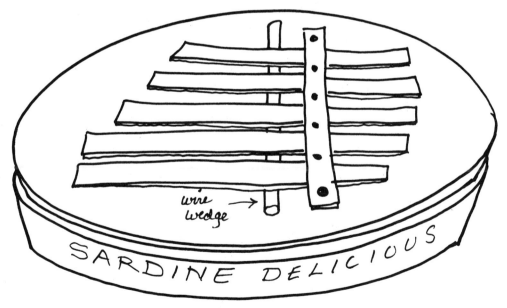

cut a tapered wooden disk to fit a sardine can—
don't worry about scale—tune by
sliding tongues and
tighten with wire wedge.

MILK CARTON GUITAR

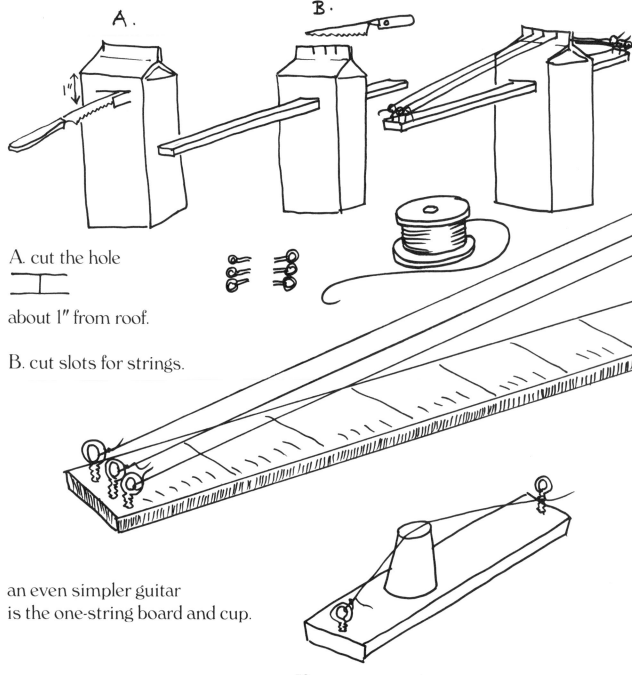

A.

B.

A. cut the hole

about 1" from roof.

B. cut slots for strings.

an even simpler guitar
is the one-string board and cup.

all you need is a yardstick,
a milk carton, six screw eyes,
a knife, and some fishing line.

If you cut this shape it will hold the stick tighter when you poke it through.

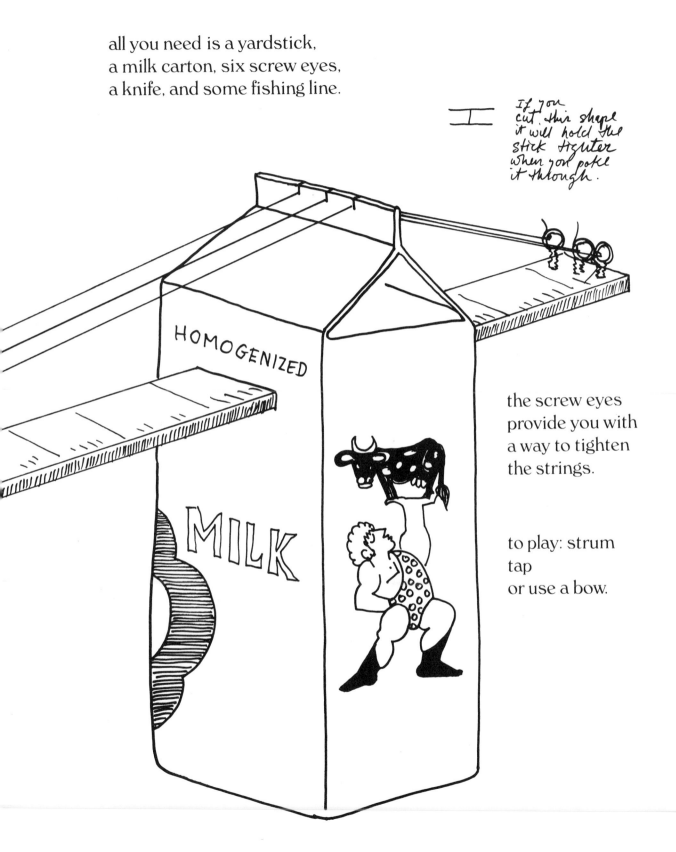

HOMOGENIZED

MILK

the screw eyes
provide you with
a way to tighten
the strings.

to play: strum
tap
or use a bow.

PLUCKING FIDDLE

this fiddle has a lovely sound.
by pressing the string down
with your thumb
you can get many very clear notes.

you need a plastic bottle,
a long stick about 1/4″ x 24″ or more
(a yardstick is fine),
two screw eyes,
a small block of wood to serve as a bridge
(a pencil will do).

saw a little ditch in the middle of
the block or pencil to cradle the string.
the string can be fishing line,
gut, or nylon monofilament.

BRIDGE

to cut holes in the bottle
so stick is tight
cut this ⊥ shape.
poke stick through.

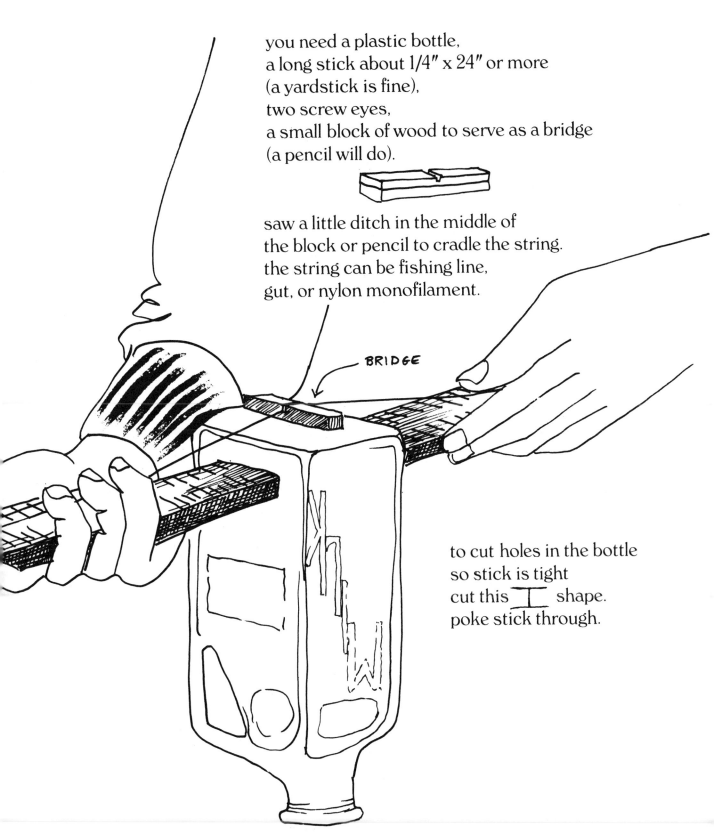

MUSICAL SAW & BOW

the common house saw
(for wood cutting)
makes beautiful music
when the bow is drawn
against the toothless edge.

I was able to order
a toothless saw directly
from the manufacturer.
The sound is the same.

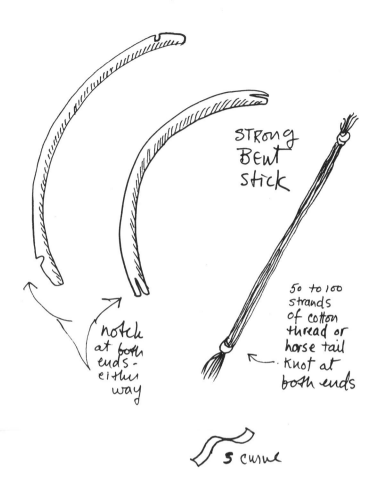

STRONG
BENT
stick

50 to 100
strands
of cotton
thread or
horse tail
↙ knot at
both ends

notch
at both
ends -
either
way

∫ S curve

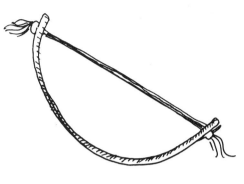

you can buy Rosin
at most music stores
to rub on bow strings
for better sound

my father once played
his musical saw in Steinway Hall in
New York City. The Reviewer said
Mr. Wiseman played his "utensil"
with skill. It was a voice & piano
solo with saw obbligato.

1. rest the saw handle against the inside of your knee, teeth
   facing inward.
2. cross your other leg over to hold the saw firmly.
3. place your thumb about 3″ from the tip and S curve the saw.
4. strike the edge firmly with a violin bow.
   with practice you can find all of the notes and play real music.
5. if you don't have a violin bow, you can tap with a stick as
   you raise the blade up and down, but you'll get no vibration.
   or, you can make your own bow from a bent stick and 50 strands
   of horse tail or cotton thread attached at both ends.
   don't forget to use rosin to make it sing.
6. the sound varies with the pressure of bow strokes:
   hard is high, and soft is low. a 28″ saw will give 6-7 notes;
   a 30″ saw will give a full octave.

WOODEN TONGUE DRUMS

every wood has its own sound.
tap a few boards and listen.
try redwood, spruce, fruit, and
mahogany for the best sounds.
at least make the top out of sonorous wood—
the rest can be pine.

58

cut top out of a hardwood (like redwood) 26" x 8".
cut two sections of piece B 6" x 8" (ends).
cut two sections of piece A 6" x 26" (sides).
cut bottom from anything 8" x 26".
there is no magic to these measurements — use what you have on hand.

a small box
will sound
higher —
a large box
will sound
deeper and
richer.

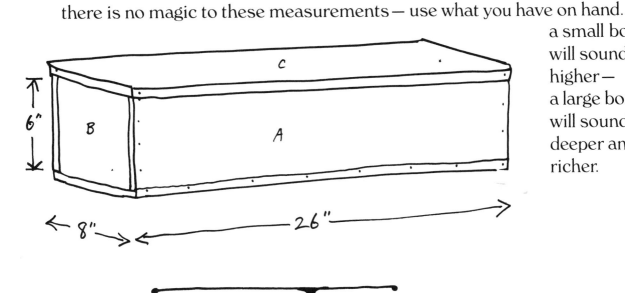

top: cut six tongues each a different length and width.
drill hole for coping saw blade to fit in.
(for drum sticks see page 19.)

HUZIX

make a square box any size:
6" x 6" or 8" x 8" x 10" x 10".
leave one side open.
cut one letter
(H . U . Z . I . X)
through the box
on each side.
use sonorous wood
for all sides.

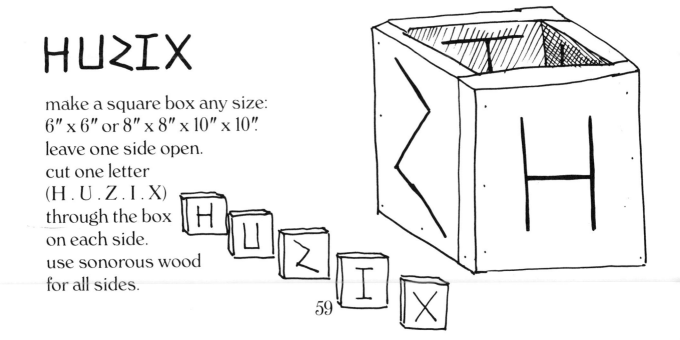

59

PAPER BAG SYMPHONY

see how many sounds
you can create
with paper bags.

shake
crumple
pop
and
bang

shake things in them
fast
slow
loud
and
soft

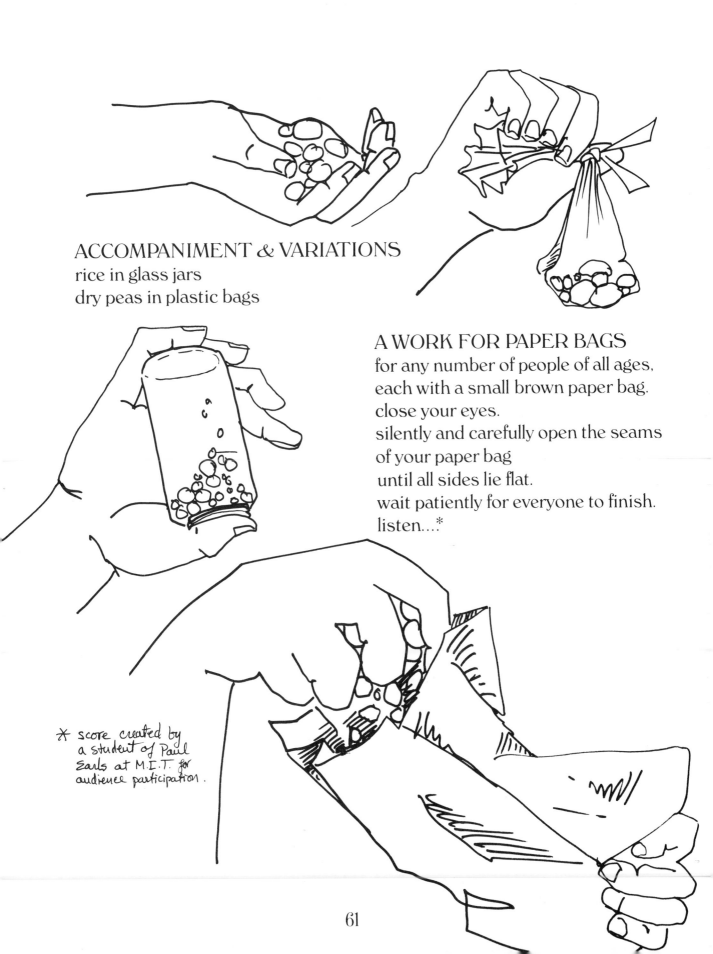

ACCOMPANIMENT & VARIATIONS
rice in glass jars
dry peas in plastic bags

A WORK FOR PAPER BAGS
for any number of people of all ages,
each with a small brown paper bag.
close your eyes.
silently and carefully open the seams
of your paper bag
until all sides lie flat.
wait patiently for everyone to finish.
listen...*

* score created by
a student of Paul
Earls at M.I.T. for
audience participation.

61

BODY SCORES

see how much sound you can get from your body. try:

clapping
tapping
clicking
picking
bumping
thumping
slapping
rapping
squeaking
blowing
ripping
scraping
puffing

BODY SCORE 1
tap your foot 1 2 3 4.
snap your fingers 1 and 3,
                        1 and 3.
whistle for a count of 2.
suck air in 3 and 4.
try it loud, soft, fast, and slow.

BODY SCORE 2
say 1 and 2 and 3 and 4.
repeat.
clap on 1 and 3.
tap foot on 2 and 4.

BODY SCORE 3
click tongue 1 2 3, pause, 1 2 3, pause (repeat).

syncopate
pat your knees on 1 2 3.
thump your chair on 4.
repeat

make up your own score.

Jelly Roll Morton was known to play the suitcase
when his drums were confiscated.

RESOURCES

This is Doug Lipman's suggested bibliography for going beyond this book into more musical adventures

A = for beginners   B = simple, but in depth   C = technical   * = especially recommended

Making Homemade Instruments

A   Whistles and Strings: Teacher's Guide. Elementary Science Study. New York: McGraw-Hill Book
*   Co., 1971. A "science unit" with ideas for open-ended exploration.

A,B   Musical Instrument Recipe Book. Elementary Science Study. New York: McGraw-Hill Book Co.,
*   1971.

A,B,C   Hunter, Ilene, and Marilyn Judson. Simple Folk Instruments to Make and Play. New York:
*   Simon & Schuster, 1977.

How to Play Instruments

A,B,C   Cline, Dallas, ed. How to Play Nearly Everything. New York: Oak Publications, 1977. Bones,
jaw harp, kazoo, handsaw, nose flute, washboard, washtub bass, jug, spoons, Irish drum.

B   Loughborough, Bill. Bongo Drum Instruction: A Rhythm Primer. Folkways Records FI 8320. For any
instrument with two sounds.

B,C   Seeger, Pete. The Steel Drums of Kim Loy Wong. Folkways Records FI 8367. Film also available.

Learning about "Real" Instruments

A   Kettelkamp, Larry. Drums, Rattles, and Bells. New York: William Morrow & Co., 1960.

_____. Flutes, Whistles, Reeds. New York: William Morrow & Co., 1962.

_____. Horns. New York: William Morrow & Co., 1964.

_____. Singing Strings. New York: William Morrow & Co., 1958.

B,C   Reck, David. Music of the Whole Earth. New York: Charles Scribner's Sons, 1977. Principles, cultural background.

Using Instruments with Children

A   Canner, Norma, ed. And a Time to Dance. Boston: Plays, Inc. (8 Arlington St., Boston, MA 02116),
1975. Photos of creative movement with retarded children. Section on instruments.

A   Hawkinson, John, and Martha Faulhaber. Music and Instruments for Children to Make. Chicago:
Albert Whitman & Co., 1969.

A   Jones, Elizabeth. What Is Music for Young Children? Washington, D.C.: National Association for
Education of Young Children (1834 Connecticut Ave., NW, Washington, DC 20009), 1969.

A,C   Hoffman, Charles. American Indians Sing. New York: John Day, 1967. Includes drum and song
record.

B,C   Biasini, Americole, Ronald Thomas, and Lenore Pogonowski. MMCP Interaction. Bardonia, NY:
Media Materials (Box 533, Bardonia, NY 10954), n.d.

B,C   Nordoff, Paul, and Clive Robbins. Music Therapy in Special Education. New York: John Day, 1971.

C   Winters, Geoffrey. Musical Instruments in the Classroom. London: Longmans, Green & Co., 1971.

Instrument Making for the Expert

B,C   Roberts, Ronald. Musical Instruments Made to Be Played. Woodridge, N.J.: Dryad Press, 1972.
*

B,C   Galloway, Margaret. Making and Playing Bamboo Pipes. Woodridge, N.J.: Dryad Press, 1971.

B,C   Schnacke, Dick. American Folk Toys: How to Make Them. Baltimore, Md.: Penguin Books, 1974.
Nine "noisemakers."

B,C   Many kits from: Peripole, Browns Mills, NJ 08015.

C   Mitchell, Howard. The Mountain Dulcimer: How to Make It and Play It—After a Fashion. Sharon,
Conn.: Folk-Legacy. 1965. Book, record.

C   Roberts, Ronald. Making a Simple Violin and Viola. N. Pomfret, Vt.: David & Charles, Inc., 1976.

C   Seeger, Pete. Steel Drums: How to Play and Make Them. New York: Oak Publications, 1964. Film
also available.

C   Wigginton, Eliot, ed. Foxfire 3. New York: Doubleday & Co., 1975. Includes information on banjos and
dulcimers.

_____, ed. Foxfire 4. New York: Doubleday & Co., 1977. Photos of mountain craftsmen.

7/3/1